D1312141

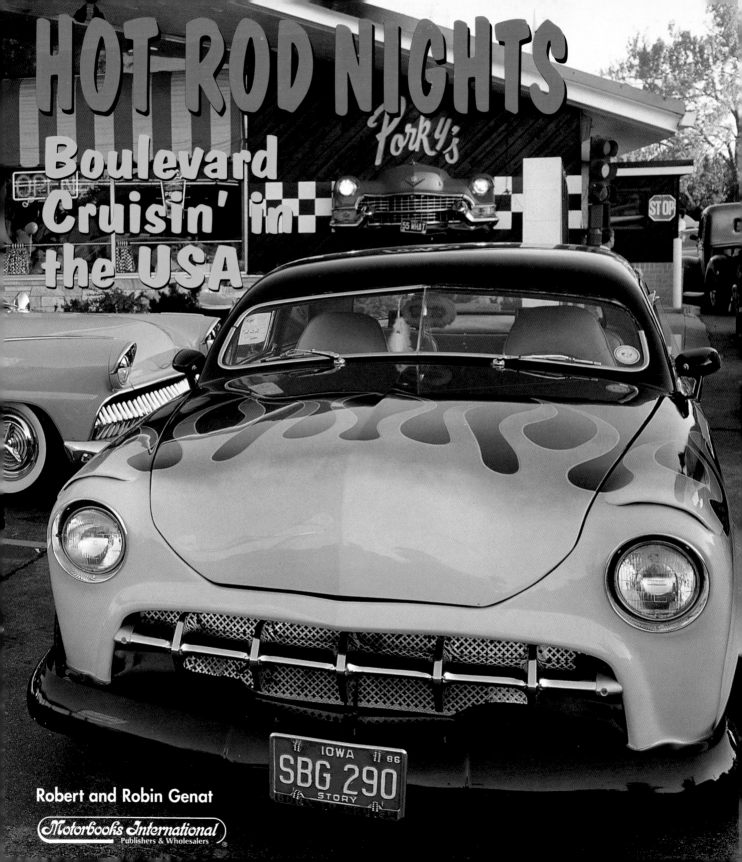

HOT-ROD NIGHTS

Boulevard Cruisin' in the USA

Robert and Robin Genat

Motorbooks International
Publishers & Wholesalers

DEDICATION

To my father, Oscar Genat.
Thanks for letting me make all those changes to
your 1963 Impala so I could look cool cruising.

First published in 1998 by Motorbooks International
Publishers & Wholesalers, 729 Prospect Avenue,
PO Box 1, Osceola, WI 54020-0001

Edited by: Lee Klancher
Designed by: Amy T. Huberty

Printed in Hong Kong through World Print, Ltd.

Genat, Robert
Hot Rod Nights: Boulevard Cruisin' in the USA /
Robert Genat & Robin Genat.
p.   cm. — (Enthusiast color series)
Includes index.
ISBN 0-7603-0288-X (pbk. paper)
1. Automobiles—United States—History. 2.
Automobiles—United States—Pictorial works.   I.
Geenat, Robin. II. Title.
III. Series.
TL23.G45 1998   97-46070
394'.3—dc21

On the front cover: Thirty years ago Oscar's drive-ins
were the hottest hangouts in Southern California.
Recently, another Oscar's chain (not related to the
original) opened and is now hosting cruise nights.
On the frontispiece: Saddle shoes and white wall tires
epitomize the retro aspect of cruising. Whether you're
16, 60, or reliving your teens, cruising the streets
holds a special appeal.
On the title page: Porky's drive-in in Des Moines,
Iowa, holds cruise nights on Wednesday and
Saturday nights from April through October. The
Saturday cruise draws more than 100 cars. There's
plenty to do for kids including limbo, hula hoop, and
ice-cream-eating contests. Adults can enter the
"suicide eating contest"—the first one to finish one of
Porky's extra-large pork tenderloin sandwiches wins
a prize. Cruising is truly a family event at Porky's.
Timothy Remus
On the back cover: The large interior of Santa
Barbara, California's, Be-Bop Burger is filled with
1950s rock 'n' roll memorabilia and its classic car of
the month, in this case, a fully-documented, one-of-a-
kind Hudson pickup.

CONTENTS

Acknowledgments

Thanks to cruisers everywhere. Cruisers spend thousands of dollars on their cars. They spend countless hours in the garage getting everything just right. On cruise night their cars are spotless. Without their craftsmanship in the automotive art and their willingness to drive their creations on a regular basis, there would be no cool cars and no cruising.

Thanks to the restaurant owners for recreating a slice of Americana for us to enjoy. Thanks for gathering all the nostalgic items that make your restaurant or diner a "blast from the past."

Special thanks to our fellow cruisers and motorheads who shared their cars and memories with us. Thanks to Tim Remus, Chris Richardson, Hans Halberstadt, and Tom Shaw for their excellent photography.

INTRODUCTION

I grew up in Allen Park, Michigan, a small suburb south of Detroit. Like most cities in the early 1960s, Allen Park had an A&W drive-in, which we affectionately called A&Dubbs. The A&W on Allen Road was about three miles from our house. It was very small and could accommodate only 20 cars. The cars parked in a horseshoe fashion around the driveway circling the small orange and brown building. Cars would enter and back into a spot on one of the three sides, leaving the driveway open between the cars and the building.

A carhop would come out with a menu and return in a few minutes to take your order. The hamburger menu was simple—you could get a Papa Burger, a Momma Burger, or a Baby Burger. The other items were standard drive-in fare: hot dogs, onion rings, and fries. You placed your order, and within a few minutes the carhop was back with a tray full of food. She'd balance the tray precariously as she walked and attach it to the window of the car when she got there. I'd never seen a burger as big as a Papa Burger or tasted one as good. The best part of eating at an A&W was the great root beer served in a heavy glass mug. On a hot, muggy summer night it was the most refreshing thing imaginable.

I'll always remember my first trip to that A&W. I was 16 years old and went with my older brother, Jim. We rode in his first car—a blue 1958 Chevy Impala hardtop. It was four years old when he bought it, but it was one of the fastest cars in our small town. It had a 348-ci engine with tri-power, a three-speed on the column, and positraction. It also had exhaust cutouts that exited at the rear edge of the front wheel opening. The stock Impala hubcaps were replaced with 1957 Plymouth hubcaps, a popular wheel-disk upgrade in the early 1960s. On the steering column was a Sun tachometer. Twin glass-packed mufflers added a throaty rumble that let everyone know this wasn't "Daddy's car." It was the kind of car every guy wanted to be seen in.

My brother taught me the fine art of cruising. He taught me how to detail a car so it would sparkle in the night lights. He explained that if I was cruising in my dad's Impala, I had to pull off the hubcaps to be cool. He demonstrated how to judiciously nurse a small Coke for an hour. He shared his secrets on finding the best parking spot in a

drive-in. He told me the proper speed to use when cruising through a drive-in. He showed me the businesses with large glass store fronts where you could catch a good mirror-like reflection of your car as you drove by—a practice known as "profiling." He showed me where all the good drive-ins and best places to drag race were located. One of the most important things he taught me was proper street racing etiquette.

By the time I got my first car (a black 1957 Chevy Bel Air hardtop), I knew where to go and how to act. There were at least eight drive-ins within a five-mile radius of my house that I regularly cruised in my Chevy. Then there were the longer trips to the Daly Drive-in on Greenfield Road in Detroit—unofficial home of the College Road Timing Association. The line of cars waiting to get into Daly's on a Friday or Saturday night stretched for a block. If you could find a place to park, you ordered the house specialty, a quarter-pound Daly Burger, fries, and a Coke—all for one dollar.

Pilgrimages to the now-hallowed grounds of Woodward Avenue, where drive-ins like Ted's and the Totem Pole were achieving legendary status, were the pinnacle of cruising pleasure. Even 30 years ago there was something special about Woodward. It was almost a religious experience for motorheads to cruise that stretch of asphalt. The mid-1960s were some of the best years of my life. And, as I've gotten older, I've found out they were magic years for a lot of my friends, too.

I was reintroduced to cruising when I bought my 1962 Chevy in 1990. One of the first places I drove to was a small 1950s diner in San Diego called Rory's. Friday nights at Rory's rocked with every imaginable type of car, from stock 1952 Chevy restorations to 1932 Ford hot rods to pro-street Nash Metropolitans. The food was greasy, but good. The live band in the parking lot played the best oldies from the 1950s and 1960s, as couples danced. I was convinced that when I restored my Chevy, it would be a driver so I could enjoy this time warp again and again.

Today, there are cruise night or cruise-in events held weekly in almost every major city across America. Nostalgia is a big part of our popular culture and cruise events allow car owners and spectators to turn back the clock to a time before the EPA throttled automotive performance and before the FDA made us feel guilty about eating a cheeseburger. So climb in and hang on—we're goin' to explore *Hot Rod Nights*.

CRUISIN' HANGOUTS

In the 1950s and 1960s, cruising to a drive-in restaurant was done for a few very simple reasons: to meet members of the opposite sex, to find someone to race, or to get something to eat. Eating was probably the least likely reason for kids to cruise, but it was the excuse for getting out of the house.

Young men seeking young women dominated the cruising scene. The car was not only the obvious mode of transportation to these meeting places but became the determining factor in establishing rank, status, and power among the guys looking for chicks. Most of the girls were glad just to have a car

The T-Bird Diner was one of the hottest cruise spots in San Diego. Every Tuesday night its lot was filled with just about every type of collector car. The T-Bird's interior was decorated with old gas pumps, gas station signs, and 1950s memorabilia. A restored pink 1957 Thunderbird sat in the middle of the dining room. Not long after this photo was taken, the T-Bird hosted its last cruise night and closed its doors to make way for a video store.

Frisco's Carhop Drive-in in Downey, California, has been serving up nostalgia by the trayful for years. Its exterior has been used as a location for several automotive magazine photo shoots. On Wednesday and Saturday nights, cars encircle the building and spill out into adjacent parking lots.

to drive and usually rolled up in the family sedan. Young men of the era, however, wanted to look cool. No Nashes or Buick four-doors, please. They wanted to drive convertibles or hardtops that in no way could be mistaken for dad's. Everyone envied the guy who drove a Corvette, a hot rod, or a muscle-car. A few guys did have cars they were fixing up, but for the most part, everyone was stuck borrowing the family car.

Kari is one of the carhops at Frisco's in Downey, California. Frisco's carhops still move about on roller skates, but they serve only the inside tables.

12

Frisco's dining room is a splash of pink, black, and white accented by neon lights. The booths are covered in pink and teal Naugahyde. An electric train on a track suspended from the ceiling whirs and toots around the diner.

Before I was able to buy my first car, I borrowed my father's new 1963 Chevrolet Impala: a dark, metallic-brown, two-door hardtop with a saddle interior. It had a 283-ci V-8 with a Powerglide transmission, but I was grateful it wasn't a six-cylinder four-door. My father was very patient with me as I tried to modify the look of his car. In exchange for this tolerance, I regularly washed and waxed his car for him. My dad never drove a dirty car. He allowed me to change the hubcaps to something more sporty. I even added a tachometer to the steering column to make it look racy. After considerable persuasion, I convinced him to let me add a Motorola reverb unit to the radio.

Reverb units were popular in the early 1960s before the introduction of FM radio. It replaced the flat sound of AM radio with a concert hall echo effect. The unit consisted of a small, fader control that mounted under the dash; one rear-seat speaker; and the unit itself,

Cruising is more a state of mind than a location. The idea is to get out and enjoy an old car and good friends. Here, a wide variety of cars from pro-street Novas to stock 1940 Ford pickups have come out to enjoy an evening at a drive-in movie.

about the size of a breadbox, which mounted in the trunk. The echo effect enhanced any song being broadcast on the radio, especially doo-wop songs already filled with echoes.

A radio with reverb was a chick magnet. If you could pull up to a carload of females, turn up the radio, and then dial in a little reverb, this new musical sound inevitably provoked interest and questions from the girls. It was the coolest ice-breaker money could buy, and best of all, the guy didn't have to be the first one to speak. Most cars attending cruise nights these days have multiwatt CD systems with several megaspeakers spread throughout the car. Many musclecar owners may have preserved the original AM radio in the instrument panel, but chances are there's a CD player hidden in the trunk.

In cruising's heyday, cruisers repeatedly drove a route that connected several desirable destinations. They didn't slow down for long and rarely even got out of their cars. Today the scene is much different. There's usually only one event held in each locale on any given night. Cruisers drive there, park the car, and spend the evening. They get out of their cars, mingle with friends, and grab a bite to eat. Today's cruisers wouldn't dream of actually eating food while sitting in the car for fear of spilling something on an immaculate interior.

Most of today's cruisers are middle-aged men who can now afford the cars they coveted as teenagers, whether they are hot rods, musclecars, or classic Corvettes. They want to turn back the clock for at least a few hours. Looking for chicks is a thing of the past. Most cruisers are married with children; some even have grandchildren. A cruise night is a great place to bring kids. Richard Weinroth, manager of Cruisers Car Wash and Diner in Northridge, California, describes his car events as "the least expensive, most wholesome hangout in Los Angeles—good, clean fun for the whole family."

In 1982 George Musser bought a hamburger joint in Pinellas Park, Florida, and turned it into Biff Burger. In 1989 Buffy's (the building on the right) was added and the 1957 Chevy was placed on the roof. Biff's hosts cruise nights for more than 200 cars every Friday night and every third Saturday night. *Tom Shaw*

Drinking and rowdy behavior is something you won't see at a cruising event. Those involved simply won't risk damaging a classic vehicle or hurting someone. Street racing is a thing of the past, too. The owners might wish they could, but the hazards and penalties are too high. In addition, pride among owners turns each one into an ambassador for the sport of cruisin'. Hot rodders might haze the tires when making an exit from a parking lot or rev the engine a little more than usual, but they're not the careless speed demons racing up and down the boulevard that they may have been as teenagers. Those who damage the reputation of the group by engaging in irresponsible and dangerous behavior are made to feel unwelcome.

Today's cruisers look for a place where they can meet friends. Locations vary from a shopping-center parking lot, a high-volume burger chain, or an independent restaurant evoking the nostalgia of the 1950s. It's good business for a restaurant to host a cruise night. A regularly scheduled cruise night brings in additional patrons for the host restaurant and results in additional revenues for other businesses nearby. The arrival of up to 100 classic cars creates excitement for everyone.

One of the largest weekly cruising events in the Pacific Northwest is in the parking lot of the Tacoma South Center in Tacoma, Washington. For the past seven years, every Saturday night from May through September, this event has drawn 200 to 300 cars. It began when a group of local hot rodders was looking for a place to meet. They approached the property manager of the center with their idea. "He was very skeptical," says Tom

The 1957 Chevy on the roof at Biff Burger was placed there in 1989. It was originally a four-door hardtop, but before placing it on the roof it was modified to its current two-door look. The paint scheme is from a 1957 Chevy that was on the cover of a late-1950s *Hot Rod* magazine. *Tom Shaw*

Andren, one of the original organizers. "He thought the worst, envisioning lots of trouble." They were given a six-week trial period with lots of rules to control those "wild hot rodders." The group had only two weeks to organize the first event, but on the first night 200 cars showed up.

At the end of the six-week trial period, the property manager was convinced this was a good idea. The event brought more people into the center, generated more revenues for the merchants, and resulted in a free car show every week. The only rule, which was implemented due to parking limitations, is that cars must have been manufactured before 1975. Car owners can park anywhere (within a roped-off area), giving the spectators a wide variety of cars in a relatively small area of the lot. Organizers take

care of security issues and, so far, there has been no trouble.

The most popular locations for cruise nights are restaurants or diners that replicate the nostalgia of the 1950s and 1960s. The T-Bird Diner, Wooly Bullys, Kooky's, Little Anthony's, Be-Bop Burgers, Jitterbugs, Boppers, and Biff Burger create their own unique versions of the past. Some exteriors are simple, with a splash of neon spelling out the name of the restaurant. Others are more elaborate, depicting giant guitars, keyboards, or something from the drawing board of a *Jetsons* cartoon. Franchise chain restaurants such as A&W, Bob's Big Boy, Dairy Queen, and McDonald's also benefit from hosting cruisers on a regular basis.

On cruise night, cars fill the parking lot of the host restaurant. Early birds arrive more

One of the things to do while waiting for your food at Biff Burger is to read the classic car want ads on the bulletin board. Biff's also has lots of entertainment for the kids during cruise nights, including creeper races and valve-cover races. *Tom Shaw*

The Tacoma South Center in Tacoma, Washington, regularly attracts between 200 and 300 cars of all types for its May through September, Saturday night cruise-ins. Cars are limited to pre-1975 models to control the size of the event. This cruise-in was started by a group of local hot rodders looking for a place to hang out.

than an hour before the scheduled starting time in order to get the best parking spots. Most locations reserve their lot for cruisers and arrange for a greeter or parking coordinator at the entrance. At some locations, participants are given a free raffle ticket for a drawing later in the evening for goods and services donated by local merchants. Half the fun is just watching the cars arrive and listening to the sound of high-performance engines.

Finding the right parking space is important. In cruiser lingo this ritual is known as

Bucks A&W in Port Orchard, Washington, overflows with more than 100 cars on its Wednesday night cruise nights. The folks in the Pacific Northwest build some beautiful cars indoors during the rainy season. Once the sun shines, they get out and drive 'em.

power parking. Each participant wants his car to be seen by the maximum number of people throughout the evening. If the cruiser is a regular, he may have his favorite place to park. Friends tend to park together. Parking is always done by backing into the chosen spot and aligning the vehicle as evenly as possible between vehicles on either side.

It's crucial to back into the space with the front end of the car facing into the lot. Leaving your hood in the closed position is a cruising faux pas and usually means you're trying to hide something. The engine compartment should be, and usually is, as clean as the rest

of the car. Because the engine is the symbol of power and status, a clean engine, well-appointed with chrome, and featuring the most horsepower-producing accessories separates the men from the boys. Engines with blowers, multiple carburetors, and pristine detailing achieve the highest regard. Dirty

The large interior of Be-Bop Burgers in Santa Barbara, California, is filled with 1950s rock 'n' roll memorabilia and its classic car of the month. This month's car is a fully documented, one-of-a-kind Hudson pickup.

20

Step up to the counter at Be Bop Burger and order from a menu that includes *The Fab Four Fish & Chips* or a *Be Bop a Lula BLT*; then wash it down with an icy Cherry Coke. The food at Be Bops is well above average; a cruising location can only go so far on nostalgia alone.

engines with leaks and evidence of poor workmanship are less likely to gain favor. A pristine 1957 Olds with a J2 tri-power engine will rate a much higher peer-approval rating than a 1969 Z-28 Camaro with a dirty engine compartment. That's just the way guys are.

Once parked, owners must anticipate and prepare for the scrutiny of the spectators. Seatbelts should not be left haphazardly on the seats, but must be aligned parallel to one another and draped perfectly over the front seat. Nothing should be left inside the car unless it's meant to enhance the nostalgic look of the interior. Any bugs meeting an

abrupt and untimely death against the windshield or grille should be swept quickly away, as with bird droppings. The owner should take a quick look along the sides and fenders for traces of spray caused by driving through a puddle of water. Some cruisers use an oversized car-duster brush to wipe down the entire car several times throughout the evening. Nighttime reflections of light on an exquisite paint job shouldn't be dulled by even the lightest layer of dust. No righteous cruiser would be caught dead with a dirty car.

Cruise nights have exposed today's car culture to many people who were unaware

The area behind the counter at Cruisers Car Wash and Diner in Northridge, California, is filled with old license plates, gas station signs, and old automotive postcards. Current car magazines are kept behind the counter for patrons to read while eating.

that hot rodders still exist. There's a sense of wonder in the eyes of spectators as they survey the brightly colored, chrome-plated old cars. After witnessing his first cruise-night event, 77-year-old Bob Creighton told me: "A few of these cars take me back 40 years! I can't believe how nice these cars are and how much money the owners have put into them."

A typical scene might be a couple strolling hand in hand along a row of cars with open hoods. When the guy discovers something unexpected—like a Hemi-powered Roadrunner—his demeanor changes visibly as he realizes what's parked in front

of him. He is alert and animated as he bends sharply at the waist and peers into the engine compartment. The woman, meanwhile, starts looking around, having spent the obligatory five seconds gazing at what appears to her as just another ordinary old blue Plymouth. Her companion pulls his head from under the hood long enough to make eye contact. As he exclaims, "It's a Hemi!" she rolls her eyes skyward and continues to scan the rest of the lot. Her hand is still in his, but by now her arm has gone limp, conveying her impatience as he continues to look into the Roadrunner's engine

Car Clubs

In the early days of hot rodding, it was common for a group of guys to get together and organize a car club. It offered these young men a social environment for their common interest: cars. It also offered them a support network for how-to mechanical advice. These clubs also allowed for tool sharing—another benefit for guys who couldn't afford the necessary equipment needed to repair or modify their cars. It wasn't unusual for someone to join a club who didn't own a car but who wanted to learn all he could about cars. Yet another benefit of club membership was the opportunity to be part of a race team. Owning a race car in the 1950s was within the financial means of a club, but beyond affordability for the average guy.

As clubs grew, so did their sense of civic involvement and responsibility. In an effort to promote a good image, clubs would fine a member who received a moving violation. The amount of the fine was usually equal to what the offender had to pay to the city or state. Clubs sponsored shows and other club events to raise money for local charities. Image building was a difficult thing

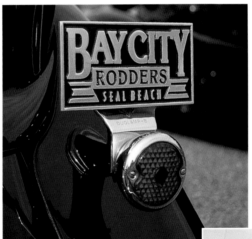

to do, because the average citizen during the 1950s was exposed to many B-movies depicting hot rodders as troublemakers.

Today's car club member is financially more secure than his 1950s counterpart. Most members have resources, knowledge, and tools to build their own cars. Clubs still promote local car shows for worthwhile charities, but rarely build or campaign race cars. Women have assumed an equal role in the clubs, and meetings are attended by both men and women. Many car clubs have women as officers, and it's not unusual to see a female club president.

It's easy to identify car club members. They still wear club jackets with the club's name embroidered on the back. These classic varsity or baseball-style jackets offer plenty of room and feature side pockets. The wearer's name is usually embroidered on the front. Worn under that jacket is a club T-shirt or other automotive-related T-shirt.

Club plaques were very popular car club items in the past. They were either displayed in the car's rear window or hung by short chains below the rear license plate. Club plaques are still quite popular on today's hot rods and add a nostalgic touch to the cars.

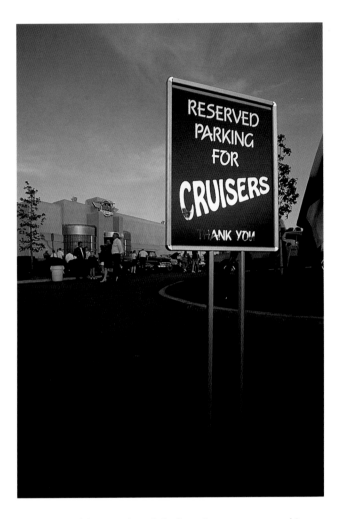

Most cruise-night locations reserve parking in their lots for cruisers only.

compartment. He soon feels the negative energy being transmitted through her limp hand. As they resume their stroll through the parking lot of classic cars, the guy turns back for one last look, and reluctantly comes down from his Hemi rush.

Drifting across the parking lot of just about any cruise night gathering is the sound of oldies music. Bill Haley & the Comets, Chuck Berry, Fats Domino, and Elvis are the predominant artists who defined an era with their 2 1/2-minute melodies. The music is friendly and usually about relationships, school, and cars. The sound system at a cruise night location may be as simple as a few speakers carrying a broadcast from a local oldies radio station, or it can be as elaborate as a live band with vocalists performing in costume. Music evokes memories of the past. In a time before MTV we created our own little "rock videos" by recalling what we were doing at the precise moment we heard a song on the radio. Our memory tapes still play today. One particular song I remember from the summer of 1963 is Leslie Gore's "It's My Party." My brother had loaned me his new black 409-powered 1963 Impala hardtop for a date.

The date consisted of me driving a pretty girl from one drive-in hangout to another in one of the hottest musclecars on the street. The song, "It's My Party," was playing when I pulled out of the A&W drive-in in Trenton, Michigan. The recollection is vivid, as if it were frozen in a photograph. I remember little else about that evening. I never really cared much for that song, but every time I hear "It's My Party," I'm immediately transported to the summer of 1963, that four-speed Impala, and that particular A&W in Trenton, Michigan. This is why oldies music is so important at any cruise night location. Memory triggers keep the past alive.

Many cruise nights feature a live band for entertainment. The high energy of a live band gets everyone moving, singing, and dancing. Today's groups and bands create names that sound like the 1950s: the Mar Dels, the Vocal Chords, the Carvelles, or the Torquays. Their theatrical costumes reflect the fads and fashion of the era: leather jackets, saddle shoes, ponytails. Surfer-style bands dress in Beach Boys fashions: light cotton pants, short-sleeved striped shirts with button-down collars, and sunglasses. You

Many cruise locations hire a local band to play during a cruise night. Here the Torquays, a Southern California surf band complete with Fender guitars and long board, have set up in the parking lot of Frisco's Carhop Drive-in in Downey.

might see matching red sport jackets when the sun goes down.

Occasionally you may find restaurants or diners that employ authentic, working carhops. Frisco's, a thriving cruise-night location in the Los Angeles area, has waitresses who navigate the interior of the restaurant on roller skates. They wear short skirts over stiff petticoats, and many of them wear knee pads. Back in the 1950s and early 1960s, more than a few young men became enamored with these delightful young ladies.

In 1960, a kid named Bob Schlotter used to hang out with his buddies at the popular Oscar's Drive-in on El Cajon Boulevard in San Diego County. The guys would spend their evenings sitting in Bob's 1959 Impala, drinking coffee, eating French fries, and watching the cars circle through. A beautiful carhop named Patti had captured everyone's attention, including Bob's. "One night," Bob recalls, "she came over to my car and said she remembered me from a high school history class. She wanted to

Previous page
Detroit is the motor capitol of the world and Wooly Bullys, in the nearby suburb of Northville, is its rock 'n' roll and cruising epicenter. Each Wednesday night during cruise season, Wooly Bullys attracts 300 to 400 cars of all types. *Chris Richardson*

A 1960 Cadillac pokes through the wall above the guitar-shaped bar at Wooly Bullys. Just in case you're wondering, the rest of the Cadillac is on the other side of the wall on the outside of the building. The car theme is also carried to the dance floor where the DJ booth is made from the front half of a 1957 Chevy. *Chris Richardson*

know if I'd mind taking her home when her shift ended."

Knowing an opportunity when he saw one, Bob agreed but became suddenly very nervous. "My Impala had tri-power, a Racer Brown cam, and a stick shift. I was so nervous when Patti got in the car, my foot was actually shaking on the clutch." They drove a few miles to another drive-in to get a bite to eat. "While I was backing into the parking space, my trembling foot slipped off the clutch! I ran into a parked car, hitting it so hard the contents of the food tray spilled into the driver's lap. What a way to impress a girl!"

Cruising need not be limited to organized events. Across the country, many car clubs get together to enjoy a drive to a local drive-in movie or to a favorite local restaurant for brunch. Groups of friends who shun the structured organization of a club consider themselves "unclubs." Someone gets an idea and just spreads the word. Pretty soon, you've got a bunch of guys going somewhere together in their old cars. Today, more than ever, enthusiasts are getting out there and driving their classic cars just for the fun of it.

HOT RODS

Loosely defined, a hot rod is a pre-1948 domestic car that has been modified for speed. The nature of those modifications is what gives the hot rod its unique look and performance.

Early hot rodders realized the value of removing the fenders from their cars. This idea dates back at least as far as Louis Schwitzer, the winner of the first race (not a 500-mile event) at Indianapolis in 1909, who removed the fenders from his Stoddard-Dayton. He noted this modification reduced weight and improved aerodynamics. The same modification was also popular with hot rod competitors at the early Southern California Timing Association (SCTA) meets at Muroc dry lake bed. Competitors would drive their cars with fenders on the city streets but remove them for competition.

Most cars designed prior to 1935 were constructed with fenders that bolted to the

This 1939 Ford coupe is covered in red and yellow flames. The faint purple glow coming from under the rocker panel is from a neon light. A current trend, the neon lights are found most often on hot rods and customs.

Larry Reda's chopped Model A Ford coupe still exhibits the characteristics that made it a great hot rod when it was built 40 years ago: a 1953 Cadillac engine, a GMC supercharger, and a very low profile.

frame or the body. As a result, they were easily removed. Without fenders, the car body sat neatly on the frame rails and took on a more streamlined racing stance. The cars built from 1935 through 1948 had rounded fenders partially integrated into the design of the body. Today's hot rodders refer to these as "fat-fendered." In recent years these fat-fendered cars have become popular. They are not as handsome with the fenders removed, but there is no right or wrong in hot rodding. It's up to the builders to express their dreams.

Fat-fendered cars bridged the gap between hot rods and custom cars. Their larger and smoother bodies offer the car builder a variety of options for his project. In

Stripped-down Model A Fords will always be a favorite of hot rodders. This chopped coupe is powered by an older Hemi engine with dual four-barrel carburetors.

the hot rod tradition, the original engine is usually replaced with something newer and more powerful. Fat-fendered cars are generally built for cruising instead of for speed. With cruising in mind, the owners want creature comforts like air conditioning and CD players. Interiors are filled with digital instrumentation, leather-covered bucket seats, and cell phones. Body modifications may include some mild customizing tricks like tunneled taillights or a sunken license plate. The large, gently curved sheet metal panels mandate excellent body restoration work and paint finish.

Hot rod engines in the 1940s and early 1950s were typically modified Chevy sixes or Flathead Fords. When the more powerful overhead-valve engines became widely available in the early 1950s, it wasn't long before they were shoehorned into the narrow early 1930s frames. No matter what engine was installed, it was modified for more power. These modifications included multiple carburetors, hotter camshafts, and low-restriction exhaust systems.

Some hot rodders still run the nostalgic Ford Flathead engine to power their hot rod. More common though are the modern small-block Chevy and Ford engines. Those dissatisfied with the mundane have opted for Chrysler Hemi or Chevrolet big-block power. Every imaginable type of modification has been made to a hot rod engine.

Driving a Hot Rod

The first time I had an opportunity to drive a hot rod I jumped at the chance. It was a full-fendered 1932 Ford roadster. The body was painted a deep maroon and the fenders were black. It had a slight rake to it, with chrome wire wheels. Power was supplied by a 302 Ford engine coupled to a Jaguar rear suspension. The first thing I noticed was the smallness of the passenger compartment. There was very little room between me and the steering wheel as I squeezed through the driver's door. It was a little difficult getting used to the interior environment, probably because it was so far removed from my daily driver or from anything else I had ever driven. The steering was also unusual. The wheel seemed awkwardly placed in relation to the seating position. It was difficult to turn and the steering gear was somewhat sloppy. The car took off like a rocket. It was nearly impossible to accelerate from a traffic light or stop sign without spinning the tires.

Driving down the freeway it hit me that I was fulfilling one of my childhood dreams. As a kid growing up in Michigan, I always dreamed of driving a 1932 Ford hot rod on a California freeway. Cruising at speed I forgot about the uncomfortable seating position and the wind buffeting around my head. I knew I looked cool in "my" Deuce roadster and was being noticed by almost everyone on the road. To the first person who gave me the thumbs up, I happily responded with a smile and big friendly wave back. The response to the car was so overwhelming (and this was in hot-rod-saturated L.A.) that within a half hour, I was just answering with a cool nod.

By the time my ride ended, I had realized the true fascination of a hot rod. Its straight-line performance is matched only by the hottest of musclecars. Its look—the combination of timeless old design and the latest in high-tech performance components—is unbeatable. The hot rod is uniquely American.

The T-Bucket

The T-bucket hot rod was brought to national attention in the 1950s when Ed "Kookie" Byrnes, America's favorite parking valet, drove his T-bucket on the television series *77 Sunset Strip*. T-buckets are the true wind-in-your-face, bugs-in-your-teeth hot rod experience. The look is extreme and exaggerated. It's the most basic of hot rods, a lightweight Model T Ford body and frame with a big engine. It's the closest thing to a dragster that can be driven on the street.

Construction of a T-bucket is simple. It begins with a pair of frame rails and a dropped front axle. The frame is modified for a late-model rear end, which is chrome plated. An original or fiberglass-reproduction 1923 Ford Model T roadster or pickup body is added. And finally, the most powerful engine available is dropped in. These engines run the gamut from small-block Chevys to Chrysler Hemis, but sometimes a Flathead Ford V-8 or a six cylinder is used. Popular induction systems include multiple carburetors on a high-rise tunnel-port intake or those same carburetors on top of a blower. The more chrome plating, the better. The exhaust headers, also chrome plated, run down the side of the car, similar to a sprint car exhaust system. The tires are exaggerated Big 'n' Littles, enhancing the car's raked stance. The total weight of one of these machines is between 1,500 and 2,000 pounds. This lightweight body and frame, propelled by an engine with over 400 horsepower, makes cruising the boulevard in a T-bucket the ultimate E-ticket ride.

This is why 1937 Fords are called "fat-fendered."

Riding in a T-bucket is a great thrill. There's very little to hang on to when these cars lurch away from a standing start.

The Deuce high-boy roadster will always be the prototypical hot rod. This one departs from a total nostalgic look by adding billet aluminum wheels and disc brakes.

Riding in a T-bucket is an experience you will never forget. There are no doors, so to enter you throw a leg over the side, making sure your other leg doesn't touch the exposed exhaust collector. If your leg does brush against the hot collector pipe, the burn you receive will always remind you to stay clear in the future. Once inside, you know you're not inside a normal vehicle. You sit *on* a T-bucket, not in it. The view out the front is of the engine and tires. Directly down to your side is the exhaust header, and just to the back is the large rear tire. Acceleration is instantaneous and vicious, and there's not much to hold onto. Catapulting off the deck of an aircraft carrier is the most similar experience that comes to mind. Response to this type of car is fantastic, especially from young kids. The T-bucket is smaller than a hot rod built from a 1932 Ford. It has copious amounts of chrome and its distorted proportions are quite appealing. A T-bucket is one of the few

"See that thing right there? That's what I need!" Cruise nights give car builders the chance to see firsthand what is being done to cars like this 1932 Ford coupe. They get the inside scoop on what owners have done to their cars during the building process.

seat-of-your-pants automotive driving experiences left in America today.

The Fenderless Model A

The fenderless Model A or 1932 Ford will always be the quintessential American hot rod. The coupe, or roadster, body style, preferably chopped, is the most traditional, and it will always catch the eye of a motorhead or first-time spectator at a cruise night.

Larry Reda of Tacoma, Washington, has had a loving relationship with his chopped Model A coupe for more than 40 years. He helped a friend build it in the mid-1950s and purchased it from that same friend in the early 1960s. "We had a lot more ingenuity than brains and more time than money— we'd try anything," Larry said. "We built a log manifold for six Strombergs from a piece

Cruise night is a time for car owners to reminisce about the good old days.

Previous page
Not all fat-fendered hot rods are Fords. This radically chopped 1940 Buick four-door sedan sports a unique set of flames. *Hans Halberstadt*

If you look closely, you can see the red custom bra the owner purchased to cover the front fenders. The bra is used on the road to prevent stones from damaging the large expanse of painted sheet metal on the fenders.

Hoods are open on cruise nights so everyone can check out the beautifully detailed engines. The owner of this Ford coupe has also hung an old drive-in restaurant tray from his door window, complete with a fake burger and fries.

of 3-inch-diameter pipe and welded it together with an acetylene torch using coat hangers for a welding rod." The coupe's 1956 Cadillac engine still runs the Chet Herbert roller cam with Studebaker adjustable pushrods that were installed in 1956. Other 1950s-era engine components are the MTC forged pistons and Nucoil dual-point, dual-coil ignition. The GMC blower was installed in 1957. It was "borrowed" one dark night from a piece of road-building equipment owned by the state of Washington.

As were many hot rods in the 1950s, this one was originally painted black primer with wide whitewall tires, red painted rims, and baby moon hubcaps. Appearance was secondary to speed. It had a reputation in Tacoma as one of the first hot rods to be a serious drag strip competitor (ETs in the low 10s) that was regularly driven on the street. "One time as I was approaching the traps at well over 100 miles per hour, the blanket we had covering the hole in the floor where the La Salle transmission sat blew off and wrapped around my face," Larry said with a laugh. "That got my attention."

Friendly waves are commonplace among hot rodders when cruising. The profile of this beautifully painted Model A coupe illustrates the classic lines of the high boy, where the body sits high upon the frame rails.

Between 1982 and 1984 Larry completely rebuilt the car with a high level of workmanship that retained the coupe's classic appearance and components. "It was time to make a decent vehicle out of it," Larry said. "I wanted to get in it, enjoy it, and have fun showin' off." Larry claims the car is very comfortable, drives exceptionally well, and visibility is deceivingly good. Washington has a fair-weather law that allows fenderless cars to be driven on the street, and Larry drives it whenever he can. "It's a car; it ain't a child. I can repaint it if it gets chipped," he said.

Larry's coupe gets a lot of attention. "You see everybody from 80-year-old ladies throwing their thumb in the air to little kids in the back seat of their parent's station wagon with their faces plastered against the window to get a better look," Larry said. "Driving it—that's the fun."

Larry Reda's classic Model A hot rod coupe proves that not all celebrated hot rods are built in huge, factory-like shops in Southern California. Great hot rods are built by ordinary individuals, and great hot rods are meant to be driven and enjoyed.

Top Cruising Car Songs

The era of rock 'n' roll coincided with the heyday of cruising. Therefore, it's not unusual that a lot of the music from the 1950s and 1960s was about cars and cruising. The following is a list of tunes that cruise-night participants often mention as their all-time favorite car songs.

Song	Artist	Hot Rod Role
"Hot Rod Lincoln"	Commander Cody and his Lost Planet Airmen	A Model A Ford races a Lincoln
"Maybelline"	Chuck Berry	An unfaithful woman and a race between a Cadillac and a V-8 Ford
"Little Deuce Coupe"	The Beach Boys	A flathead-powered 1932 Ford hot rod
"409"	The Beach Boys	An unstoppable 409-powered 1962 Impala
"Shut Down"	The Beach Boys	A race between a Sting Ray and a 413 Dodge
"No Particular Place to Go"	Chuck Berry	Playing the radio and cruising
"Little GTO"	Ronnie and the Daytonas	An anthem to the GTO
"Dead Man's Curve"	Jan & Dean	A race between an XKE Jaguar and a Corvette
"Fun, Fun, Fun"	The Beach Boys	Cruising in daddy's T-Bird instead of studying at the library
"Little Old Lady from Pasadena"	Jan & Dean	A red Super Stock Dodge and the elderly woman who owns it
"Mustang Sally"	Wilson Picket	A woman who won't slow down in her Mustang

This 1932 Ford high-boy roadster has a nostalgic paint scheme based on the dry-lakes racers of the 1930s and 1940s. The small cylinder in front of the grille is a fuel tank typical of those used by dry-lake racers.

Hot Rod Glossary

Big 'n' Littles: The time-honored hot rod tradition of smaller front tires and larger rear tires, adding to the overall raked look of the car.

Chopped: Lowering the roofline by cutting sections out of the roof pillars.

Coupe: An enclosed two-passenger body style produced through 1948.

Deuce: All hot rods built from a 1932 Ford.

Fat fender: A hot rod built from a car produced between 1935 and 1948, named for its large rounded fenders.

Flathead: The first V-8 engine widely used in vintage hot rods. It was first produced in 1932 and last installed in a production Ford product in 1953. It is named for the flat design of its cylinder heads.

Full-fendered: A hot rod with the original factory fenders covering all four wheels.

High boy: A late-1920s through early-1930s hot rod that has not had the body channeled over the frame rails.

Low boy: A late-1920s through early-1930s hot rod with its body channeled over the frame rails to lower the overall profile.

Rake or raked: A car with a lowered front end.

Roadster: An open two-passenger body style, similar to a convertible without roll-up windows; produced until 1936.

T-bucket: A hot rod built with Model T Ford body and devoid of fenders and hood.

This pretty blue T-bucket proves there are no hard-and-fast rules in hot rodding. Most T-buckets have V-8 engines, but this one breaks the mold by running a straight six-cylinder engine.

The body on this 1946 Ford convertible is completely stock and has been expertly restored. All of the modifications are under the skin with the exception of the radial tires and mag wheels.
Hans Halberstadt

CUSTOMS

Following World War II, many servicemen who returned to the United States via the West Coast decided to settle in California. They needed cars to drive, but new cars were scarce. So they bought used Fords and Chevys from the mid-1930s through the early 1940s.

The young car owners wanted to individualize their older cars so they made subtle modifications. By simply changing a few design features, guys were creating their own "new cars." They swapped grilles and bumpers with parts from more expensive models, giving their used cars a sleeker look. They also lowered the cars, swapped the hubcaps, removed the chrome trim, and repainted. These modified cars were some of the first to sport the new metallic colors of the late 1940s. This was the advent of the custom car. They got styling cues from other customs and the new production cars.

The young lad in the foreground is gazing up at the chopped top of a 1949 Merc lead sled. This particular custom is painted in two shades of suede. There is nothing on this car that couldn't have been installed in the 1950s.

A four-door isn't the most popular body style for a custom car, unless its a 1949 Merc. A two-door body style is normally preferred for a great custom look. But because the Merc is so distinctive from a design standpoint, the four-door still looks good when customized. *Hans Halberstadt*

The Barris brothers, Sam and George, were the kings of the early California customs. They started customizing cars in the late 1930s. Word of mouth brought them business, and following the war they opened their own shop. Sam was an expert in metal crafting and was soon chopping tops and sectioning bodies. In the late 1940s the burgeoning automotive enthusiast magazine industry recognized the brothers' talent and started to feature their work. This increased their business and encouraged others to start their own customizing shops.

About this same time, a new car was introduced that would become an icon for the customizing world—the 1949 Mercury.

Its inverted-bathtub styling lent itself to the customizing tricks of the day. It begged to be chopped and lowered. The Barris brothers wasted no time in reworking the Merc into a classic style known as the lead sled. The ultimate of all classic Barris Merc customs was Bob Hirohata's 1951 Merc. He asked to have the B-pillar removed when it was chopped for a hardtop look. What the Barris brothers created was a car with clean classic proportions. Hirohata's Merc set the tone for the customizing world. Its look, style, and proportions have been repeated in hundreds of custom cars.

By the time the 1950s rolled around, car design had changed. Fenders were integrated

This 1956 Ford Victoria hardtop is an excellent example of a mild custom. It features a nosed hood, spinner hubcaps, and rear fender skirts. This type of custom was popular in the 1950s, and its nostalgic look adds to any cruise night.

into the design of the body, and hardtop styling was available on all but a few models. Engine technology had also improved, so the new cars ran as well as they looked. The 1950s were the heyday of custom cars. It was rather simple to modify any car into a custom by nosing, decking, lowering, and adding a set of spinners. Other subtle touches added to the look. Appelton spotlights, fender skirts, full-length Lakes Pipes running along the rocker panel, and custom taillight lenses are examples of customizing features.

Customs were made for those who wanted to cruise low and slow. The engines might be mildly reworked for a little extra performance but not to the level of the hot rodder.

The idea was to look cool, cruise comfortably, and enjoy your dates. Necker knobs were added to the steering wheel, so the driver could keep his right arm around his favorite girl and still be able to steer the car easily, with his left hand, without power steering.

With today's "anything goes" attitude toward cruising and the love of nostalgia, the custom car has made a big comeback. It offers the owner a highly styled nostalgia machine that is as comfortable and, in most cases, better looking than any Lexus or Mercedes on the road. Many of today's customs roll on a newer chassis or on subframes offering upgraded suspension geometry and an improved ride. The interiors of today's customs are fitted

Lowered 1956 Mercurys make cool cruising customs. This one features full-length Lake pipes, spinner hubcaps, and Appelton spotlights. The door handles have been shaved. The doors open by pushing a small hidden button that actuates a solenoid and unlatches the door lock.

with rolled-and-pleated, leather-covered, split-bench seats with six-way power controls. Digital instrument panels, CD players, and cruise control complete the interior. A few of today's customs have taken a lesson from low riders and have installed hydraulic suspension controls to lower their cars as much as possible when parked. When it's time to drive away, the hydraulic suspension raises the car to a safe driving position.

The overall look of the custom has not changed much since the 1960s. The cars are still low and sleek. Modern paints, however, have added a new level of visual distinction. Years ago, the only paint available was a solid or a metallic color. When the Barris brothers invented Candy Colors, it set the automotive

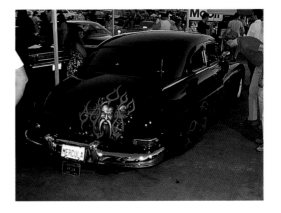

"Mercula" is another 1949 Mercury that has a super-low stance. Its full-height roofline is unusual, because most early Merc customs are chopped.

world on end. Today the look is highly finished in a multitude of solid, two-tone, or multicolored shades. Some still feature the ever-popular flames. One of the popular paint schemes today is created through the use of colored primers: This finish is called suede. Hot rod black primer once was the color of choice on a car under construction. Today we are likely to see a custom sedan at a cruise night in one of several shades of primer.

Many lead sleds from the 1940s and 1950s have been resurrected and restored to their original condition. And many new customs have been built in an effort to recreate the traditional look of the original Barris-built customs. Cruising in a custom is a real treat—it catches everyone's eye. Unlike a hot rod or musclecar, the custom car cruiser is not a racer. He sits low and goes slow, giving everyone a chance to see his rolling piece of sculpture.

The blue suede 1959 Ford in the foreground was customized in the early 1960s. Its body has been sectioned and the car has been lowered. The stock 1959 Ford in the background provides an interesting comparison.

Cat's Eye headlight shields and louvered hoods are two of the many small details added to custom cars.

Customs have always been associated with a bad-boy image. They gained widespread notoriety with the movie *Rebel without a Cause*, starring James Dean. In that movie Dean drove a customized 1949 Mercury coupe that was nosed, decked, and wore fender skirts. No one was cooler than James Dean, and every guy wanted to look like him, act like him, and drive a car like his.

American Graffiti also connected cruisers with delinquent types. At one point in the movie, Richard Dreyfus was held hostage by members of the Pharaohs car club and was coerced into committing misdemeanors while cruisin' around in a chopped 1951 Merc. The Pharaohs wore their hair long and slicked back. They had the obligatory car club jackets and the look of guys who belonged in reform school.

The bad boy image is indelibly linked to custom cars, but the owner of one of these classics today is likely to be anything but a fringe member of society. These cars now hold a special place in the history of hot rodding and owners invest substantial amounts of money and time on them.

The differences between customs and low riders can be subtle. They both share an extremely low stance. This particular 1963 Chevy Impala low rider has cruiser skirts covering the rear wheel openings. The low rider generally has very wide wire wheels with thin-line tires; the custom frequently has wide whites with hubcaps. The interiors of low riders tend to be more ornate than the custom's simple tuck 'n' roll trim.

This 1957 Ford convertible could have been built in the 1950s and stored in a time capsule for us to enjoy today. It is lowered, has full-length Lake pipes, spinner hubcaps, cruiser skirts, twin-tunneled antennas, and a white tuck 'n' roll interior. *Timothy Remus*

This 1940s-era Cadillac has been turned into a stunning custom. It has been chopped and lowered and features large-diameter mag wheels—perfect for a summer night's cruise.

Diner Decor

Many of today's cruise-night locations center around a 1950s-era diner or restaurant. Although many popular fast-food chain restaurants sponsor cruise nights, it's the independent restaurant owners who create a special feeling of nostalgia for their customers.

These restaurants are open, bright, and bursting with activity. They offer counter seating, booths to seat small parties of two or four, and large tables that can seat up to eight or ten guests. The kitchen area is often visible to customers. There's lots of hollering back and forth, calling out new orders and announcing orders ready for delivery to hungry guests. Food is served on heavy-duty, white porcelain dishes or in red plastic, open-weave baskets lined with waxed paper. Or if customers order first and then pick up the food at another counter, they might be given a name, instead of a number. " 'Little Darlin" and 'Road Racer,' your orders are ready!"

Food servers are often in costume, recreating the look of the 1950s and 1960s: saddle shoes, cat-eye glasses, big hair, and serious gum chewing. A few restaurants still hire young people to "carhop," inside and out, on a pair of roller skates, complete with knee pads and elbow guards. At some diners, food servers may spontaneously burst into song and dance to entertain guests. We've seen some very authentic waitresses "of a certain age" dressed in snappy uniforms, sensible shoes, and starched caps.

The details of the interior decor reflect what was fashionable in the 1950s and 1960s. Favorite color schemes are red, white, and black; and pink, turquoise, and black. The black-and-white checkered pattern is also a favorite theme, usually for the floor. Tables, chairs, booths, counters, and stools are made of Formica, trimmed in chrome, and covered in vinyl materials. Booths may often be upholstered to look like tuck and roll, with piping in a contrasting color, or with "buttons and biscuits."

The walls are covered with murals, photos, posters, and unique displays of memorabilia. Artwork depicts movie stars (James Dean), musical groups (Beach Boys, Jan & Dean, Chuck Berry, Elvis), movies ("Psycho" and "Attack of the Fifty Foot Woman"), and classic cars of the 1950s and 1960s. Near the entrance, a life-size photo of Marilyn Monroe may beckon you to "Please Wait to be Seated." Autographed black-and-white 8x10 glossies of celebrities seem to be everywhere, as do framed front pages of newspapers with memorable headlines.

Interesting items may also be hanging from the ceiling, like a working electric toy train. A few restaurants display a classic car inside. Even a trip to the rest room can be nostalgic. Take the hall marked "Memory Lane" and choose the appropriate door: "Cool Cats" or "Cool Chicks." You may also find large working props like the cheesy self-portrait photo booths (four photos for $2 while you wait) or displays of surfboards and vintage electric guitars.

Music—from the 1950s and 1960s—is the final touch. Some restaurants feature a DJ on busy nights of the week; some have a jukebox from which customers can select their favorite tunes; others may simply turn on the local or regional Oldies radio station. On special occasions, the owner may hire a band. The kids always wonder why the older people know all the words!

Custom Car Glossary

Appeltons: Spotlights mounted on the cowl; named for the manufacturer.

Channeled: Lowering the body over the frame rails to create a sleeker overall vehicle profile.

Chopped: Lowering the profile of a passenger-car greenhouse by cutting a few inches out of the roof pillars.

Floating grille: Grille bars or teeth that are mounted from behind and appear to be suspended within the vehicle's grille opening.

Frenched: The process of recessing components such as taillights, license plate, antenna, or headlights into the vehicle's body.

Lake pipes: Chrome exhaust pipes that run the full length of the rocker panel.

Lead sled: A name routinely used to describe all 1949–1951 Mercury customs. It describes a custom car that has had several major body modifications, such as sectioning or chopping. The term comes from the quantity of lead used as a body filler on customs built in the 1950s.

Lowered: A car that has been brought closer to the ground by a modification to the front and rear suspension.

Mild custom: A car that has a few minor body modifications, such as a shaved hood and deck. It may be lowered and will most certainly have nonstock hubcaps.

Olds fiestas: A three-bar spinner hubcap manufactured by Oldsmobile and embraced by early customizers.

Radical custom: A car that has extensive chassis and body modifications, such as chopping, sectioning, or extending the fenders.

Sectioned: An extensive process of removing a few inches in height from a vehicle's body, creating a vehicle with a very low profile.

Shaved: Removal of chrome trim items like hood ornaments, deck lid emblems, or door handles.

Skirts: Smooth sheet metal panels added to cover the car's rear wheel openings. Larger skirts that extend to the rear bumper are often called "cruiser skirts."

Slammed: Extreme lowering of a vehicle by altering both the suspension and frame.

Tuck 'n' roll: Pleated custom interior very popular in the 1950s and 1960s.

Tunneled: See Frenched.

CHAPTER 4

MUSCLECARS

The 1960s musclecar boom sucker-punched the custom car craze. Why cruise slow when you can go fast in factory iron? Musclecars had the interior room of a custom and the performance of a hot rod. By the mid-1960s, custom cars were scarce at the drive-ins. They had been replaced by high-horsepower Chevelles and GTOs.

In its most simple form, the term "musclecar" refers to a factory-built high-performance car. The debate over what date marks the beginning of the musclecar era will rage forever among motorheads and automotive historians. Some believe the era of the musclecar started in the late 1950s when Chevrolet's fuel-injected 283-ci engine was offered in the full-size Bel Air. Others say it was when Chrysler's 1957 300C, with its dual-quad Hemi motor, cranked out 390 horsepower. Still others say musclecars were born when the 100-miles-per-hour mark was broken in the quarter-mile by a passenger car running in

Tim Stout's cruise night car is a 1968 Chevelle 396SS that he bought from his grandfather in 1981. After a few years of cruising and racing it on the streets, Tim restored it to its original appearance.

1962 Chevy Bel Air bubbletops with 409-ci engines set the drag strips and streets on fire in the early 1960s. Immortalized in song by the Beach Boys, 409 Chevys will live in the hearts of motorheads and classic Chevy lovers forever.

a stock class. This would include cars like the 1959 Pontiac Catalina, which ran the quarter-mile in 13.91 seconds at 102 miles per hour.

The Big Three auto manufacturers were building and featuring high-performance engines in 1960, somewhat under the guise of "police specials." At the same time, interest in NASCAR racing was spreading, and each manufacturer wanted to see its car in the winner's circle. Interest in the NHRA stock car classes was growing even faster. By 1962 each of the Big Three was offering cars that—off the showroom floor—would easily surpass the 100-miles-per-hour mark in the quarter-mile.

Performance cars of the early 1960s were based on the full-size passenger car. While the engines generated a lot of horsepower, they also had a lot of iron to move. A car of that era could weigh up to 4,000 pounds. Two things happened in 1964 to change that trend: Ford introduced the Mustang, and Pontiac released the GTO. Both cars were based on a lightweight body with a high-performance engine. These cars sold well, in part, because of the lower sticker price compared to a full-size sedan with a high-performance engine. It wasn't long before every manufacturer was selling a lightweight performance car. By the end of the 1960s the advertised horsepower ratings had leveled off, but vehicle performance was skyrocketing.

This continued escalation in horsepower was evident on the streets, as cars fresh from the showroom were taking on and beating some of the fastest hot rods in town. It begged the question: Why spend years building a hot rod when you could go to your local new car dealership and order a factory musclecar? All it took was a few minutes to check off the desired options on the order sheet, put a few

It doesn't have to be a Ford, Chevy, or Mopar to be a true musclecar. This American Motors AMX earned its musclecar stripes in the late 1960s and early 1970s by beating some of the best. Judging by the smile on the owner's face, it must be a fun car to drive.

dollars down, and wait the usual six weeks for delivery. The customer soon had a custom-built race car with a warranty! Some dealers got wise and pulled the customer aside for a bit of advice at the time of delivery. The young buyer was warned not to expect more than one engine, one clutch, or one transmission under the warranty.

Tim Stout owns one of the finest examples of the musclecar era—a 1968 Chevelle 396SS. Tim has owned this car since 1981, when he bought it from his grandfather for $2,000. Tim's grandfather wanted a family car with lots of power for the highway, automatic transmission and power steering for ease of driving, and air conditioning for those trips across the hot southwest desert. No bucket seats for grandpa; he ordered a bench seat so all the grandchildren could ride along in comfort.

In 1981 gas prices were rising, Tim's grandfather was ready to sell the Chevelle in favor of something more economical, and Tim was looking for his first car. He was in high school and his criteria were simple: a car that would impress his friends and a car that he could race. He was looking for a Nova and never even considered the Chevelle. At his grandfather's suggestion, Tim took a short test drive and was convinced this was the car for him.

Tim and his buddies hung out at a local Jack in the Box restaurant in Lemon Grove, California. "We'd meet at Jack in the Box, pop the hoods on the cars, and everybody would start bragging," Tim said. "Everybody would pair off and then go out to Imperial Avenue where we had a quarter-mile marked by painted lines on the street. My first race was against a 1969 396SS Chevelle

The Z/28 Camaros, like this 1968 model, were very popular in their day. They had a highly refined small-block Chevy engine and a superb chassis. Chevrolet advertised them as "the closest thing to a Corvette yet."

that had a four-speed transmission. He was the 'big king' at school and I thought he had a pretty fast car. He'd beaten most everybody and I was the only one he hadn't raced. We went down to Imperial and I beat him by four cars. When we got back to Jack in the Box, he wouldn't say too much about it. I felt pretty good and it gave me bragging rights for a couple months until somebody kicked my ass. There will always be someone to come along who's faster."

After more than a year of thrashing it on the street and down the strip, Tim decided to restore his Chevelle. He did most of the work himself, leaving only the machining of the engine and the painting to the experts. He agonized over the suggestions of his friends: Paint it red, modify the engine, put headers

on it. Logic took over and Tim restored his Chevelle to original condition. Tim Stout's Palomino Ivory 1968 396SS Chevelle stands out as a unique 1960s musclecar. He regularly drives to cruise nights and car shows.

For extended cruising, a musclecar has several advantages over almost any other car. First and foremost is its interior room. Except for the smaller Camaros and Mustangs, the average musclecar can easily carry four to six people. Leg room abounds in the front and rear seats of the larger-bodied cars like Road-runners and Chevelles. Factory options like power steering and power brakes bring up the comfort level even more. Those lucky enough to find a musclecar with air conditioning have found the ultimate in cruising—sit back, relax, and enjoy the cool ride. Few musclecars were optioned with air conditioning, however, since most performance enthusiasts wanted pure horsepower, not accessories that drained power from the engine.

The era of the musclecar was also the era of street racing. Anyone with a down payment could own the fastest car on the boulevard. Racing is also what led to the decline of the musclecar era because of high insurance rates. Nowadays, most musclecars are owned by middle-aged men living out the dreams of their youth. They rarely street race. The penalty of getting a ticket or damaging their expensive restoration serves as a potent deterrent.

Greg Rager was a young man in the early 1960s in Johnstown, Pennsylvania. He hung out at the Jolly Roger drive-in located in Richland Township, Pennsylvania. The car he drove was his mom's 1959 Pontiac

Pulling up to a stoplight next to a Plymouth Roadrunner that looked as good as this one would always give street racers a little tingle up the spine.

The 454 Chevelle Super Sport was the ultimate musclecar for Chevy fans. This beautiful red hardtop has a cowl-induction hood and aftermarket mag wheels.

This red 1964 Plymouth is reminiscent of the cars that ran in Super Stock class at the drags in the early 1960s. The five-spoke mag wheels and the wide rear tires set off this musclecar perfectly.

Catalina four-door sedan. It was powered by a 389-ci engine with a two-barrel carburetor, single exhaust, and a three-speed stick on the column. "I was driving a stick-shift Pontiac and I was hot stuff, even though it had four doors," Greg said. Street racing often was launched from the Jolly Roger and young Greg participated whenever he could. "The car was ill-equipped to handle the power shifts I was making," Greg admitted. "I tore three transmissions out of that car, and every time my mom would ask me if I'd been racing, I'd deny it."

Like a lot of young men during the 1960s, Greg joined the Navy for a four-year stint. When he returned to Pennsylvania, he bought a 1961 Chevy Super Sport. "I can puff my chest out and say that I owned one of the few original 1961 Super Sports. While it was

In 1970 the performance version of the Plymouth Barracuda was called simply the 'Cuda. It was offered with a variety of engines including the 425-horsepower Hemi. This particular 'Cuda has a 440-ci engine and an outstanding paint job.

a nice car, it was five years old and was no longer competitive with the new 1966 396SS Chevelles and GTOs," Greg said. "So in 1967, I sold it and bought a year-old GTO."

In 1969, while he was working at a Chrysler-Plymouth dealership as a mechanic, Greg ordered a new Plymouth GTX. It was Ivy Green with a black interior and powered by a 440 engine with a four-speed transmission. "The first night I had the car I babied it, never taking the engine over 2,000 rpm," Greg said. "That weekend I took it on a trip to Columbus, Ohio, to visit a relative. While I was there, I took it to the drag strip. I remember it caused quite a stir, since not many people had seen a new GTX. I also remember I ran a 14.3 with it."

During his GTX years, Greg was hanging out at Stuver's drive-in and most of his buddies had musclecars. "There was a little bit of everything: 428 Cobra Jet Torinos, 396 Chevelles, Roadrunners, Olds 442s, and a Buick Grand Sport," Greg said. "We used to race in Babcock Park, where we had the quarter-mile marked out on the street. Then a new section of four-lane, limited-access road that ran from Evansburg to Sommerset opened up about two miles from Stuvers. On that road was the McNally bridge—a street racer's dream. It was *exactly* 1,320 feet of new concrete. At each end was a 20-foot section of asphalt that was perfect for burnouts.

"I had one of the fastest cars around, but I was always tinkering with it at the dealership." Greg got the reputation as the "high-performance wrench" at the dealership and was tuning all the Chrysler-Plymouth police cars and the other hot cars that were sold. "There were times when I'd be tuning a car owned by a guy I'd just beaten the night before. Most of the time the owner of the car didn't even know I was working on his car. I'd always do a good job, because that guy might be up against a Chevelle and I wouldn't want him to lose."

The Ford Mustang is an extremely popular car with cruisers. Restoration and high-performance parts are readily available for all years. The GT 350 Shelby Mustang was available in 1965, powered by a high-performance 289-ci engine. It was intended for the road-race set, but many street racers liked them too. *Chris Richardson*

One race Greg remembers well was against a 343 Javelin. In the late 1960s, American Motors was heavily involved in racing. AMC didn't have a big engineering budget, so it purchased off-the-shelf, high-performance parts like intake manifolds, carburetors, cams, and headers from the aftermarket

1950s Food Served Today

In the 1950s and 1960s, menu choices were rather simple and, as we look back, inexpensive. Most of the larger drive-in chains had their own specialty burger. A&W had the Papa, Momma, and Baby Burger lineup. Big Boy had, and still has, the famous double-decker with their special sauce. The smaller chains and independents each had their own specialty burger, too. The Totem Pole was a small independent drive-in on Woodward Avenue in suburban Detroit and offered the Big Chief Burger—a double-decker with special sauce. In 1960 the Daly drive-in chain had 11 locations in southeastern Michigan. Their menu listed a total of 26 items. At the top was their quarter-pound Dalyburger, which, of course, had its own variety of special sauce. The most expensive item on the Daly menu was the chicken dinner at $1.35. It included French fries, cole slaw, and a roll with butter. The least expensive item on the menu was a 10-cent cup of coffee. The food was tasty and plentiful and nearly everything was fried. But back then, cholesterol levels were of no concern.

Today's 1950s-style cruise-night hangouts offer a broader selection of food, much of which is more healthy than what was offered in the past. Turkey Burgers, Veggie Burgers, and a variety of good garden greens from the Tossin' and Turnin' salad bar are available for those looking for nutritional value and a clear cardio-vascular system. Today, food is available on whole wheat bread and even pita pocket bread, unknown in the America of the 1950s.

Each diner or restaurant still has a specialty burger made from ground beef with a name somehow attached to the past. Some of my favorites are the Be-Bop Burger, Chubby Checker's Chili Cheeseburger, and the ever popular Frankie and Annette Burger. Other favorites include "Beaver Cleaver's" Tri Tip Beef sandwich, "La Bamba" Chili, and the "Flipper" fish sandwich. Save room for dessert so you can order a "Banana Fanna Moe Manna" Banana Split.

Duggan's Irish Pub in Royal Oak, Michigan, has revived a piece of Woodward Avenue cruising history by recreating the Big Chief Burger, originally served up by the Totem Pole drive-in. Owner Larry Payne personally blends the Big Chief's secret sauce from the original recipe. Close your eyes, bite down, and it's 1963 again with nostalgia you can smell and taste. Along with its great burgers, Duggan's has become the unofficial Totem Pole Museum. Its walls are decorated with photographs and memorabilia from one of Detroit's hottest cruising spots in the 1960s.

The Big Chief Burger: two large beef patties with cheese, pickles, and special sauce. It was originally served up by the Totem Pole drive-in on Woodward Avenue. *Tom Shaw*

Muscle Car Glossary

Dual-quads: Dual four-barrel carburetors, de rigueur for the hottest musclecars.

Fuel injection or FI: In the 1950s and 1960s, it referred to the Rochester (mechanical) version on Corvette 283- and 327-ci engines.

Goat: A Pontiac GTO.

Hemi: The baddest of bad musclecar engines; developed by Chrysler, named for its hemispherical combustion chamber; a Hemi-powered musclecar is the Holy Grail of all musclecars.

Hurst: Sturdy replacement shifter-linkage for four-speed transmissions; used by the most ardent racers.

Pony car: A musclecar based on Ford's Mustang or Chevrolet's Camaro.

Ram inducted: A dual four-barrel intake manifold with very long internal passages perfected by Chrysler in the early 1960s.

Six-pack: Three two-barrel carburetors as seen on a Chrysler product.

Super stocker: A generic name for early musclecars. Super stock was the name of the drag racing class the NHRA designated for passenger cars with high-performance engines.

Tach: Shortened term for tachometer, a gauge that indicates the engine's crankshaft revolutions.

Tri-power: Three two-barrel carburetors as seen on Fords, Pontiacs, Oldsmobiles, Chevrolets, and Corvettes.

289-302-351-390-406-427-428-429: Cubic-inch displacement for various Ford musclecars.

340-383-413-426-440: Cubic-inch displacement for various Mopar musclecars.

389-421-400: Cubic-inch displacement for various Pontiac musclecars.

302-327-350-396-409-427-454: Cubic-inch displacement for various Chevrolet musclecars.

manufacturers and added AMC part numbers. This particular Javelin had been a demonstrator owned by the dealer's son. It was loaded with all the factory speed equipment. "I had been mouthing off and this guy finally had enough of me. Right out of the hole he had a fender on me and held it all the way. He offered to go again, but I told him no; he beat me fair and square." Today, Greg still owns that GTX, which has a total of only 14,000 miles on it.

If you were to ask a musclecar owner why he owns that particular car, he would probably have some specific answers for you. He might remember the first one he saw when the car was new. He might mention the name of the coolest guy in his hometown high school who owned this car. He might remember a specific race where this car beat the "King of the Hill" back in high school. The guy who drives a musclecar to a cruise night today didn't necessarily buy it because it was a good financial investment. He probably bought it to relive a little of the past and to become "King of the Hill."

The Unusual and Ordinary

Most cars that frequented the drive-ins during the 1950s and 1960s were owned by the parents of the young cruisers. Teenagers, who were glad to have anything to drive, packed the drive-ins with station wagons and inexpensive two-door and four-door sedans. Few kids could afford the attention-getting hot rods, Corvettes, and musclecars.

Until recently, the trend at cruise nights was toward highly individualized hot rods, customs, and modified cars. Lately, however, cruise nights have been attracting more ordinary four-door sedans and stock restorations. They may not have a big engine or custom wheels, but they bring a true taste of nostalgia to a cruise night by representing what most of us drove 30 years ago when these cars were new.

What could be more fun than driving down the street with your best girl by your side in a fully restored 1962 Impala convertible? Convertibles make great cruisers. Just ask anyone who owns one.

The 1955 Chevy is one of the all-time great street machines. The two-door sedan in a pro-street configuration is extremely popular today. This particular Chevy has been tubbed, has a roll bar installed, and has a fuel cell in the trunk.

The owner of a fully restored car will not get the attention from those with a need for speed, but he will certainly get the attention of the motorhead who loves all forms of the American automobile. The restored car also gets its share of attention from the average citizen, who recognizes the four-door sedan or station wagon restoration as something he, his parents, or a relative once owned. Fortunately, more restorers are bringing these cars out to cruise nights for everyone to see.

Prime It and Drive It

Cars in primer (the flat base coat of paint, usually black, applied to sheet metal) were common in the 1950s. Just owning a car that was drivable was a feat for most young men. Paint was something that they could add later, when they scraped enough money together, and was always less important than a cam or carburetors. Today, and probably forever, cars will be driven in primer. It's still the symbol of a work in progress and has become an automotive fashion statement as well. The "suede" finishes—named for their resemblance to napped leather—come in all colors and are most often seen on hot rods and customs. Some upscale cruise locations have attempted to exclude cars in primer, but in doing so, have felt the wrath of their local hot rod community. Forty years ago, nearly every young man's car was painted in primer at some point.

Some people even trailer their race cars to a cruise-night event. These will usually be full-bodied Chevelles or Mustangs, but don't be surprised to see any type of competition car. The owner will usually fire it up with open exhaust and drive it from the trailer into a parking location. The sound of the open exhaust reverberating among the surrounding buildings will always attract a crowd. As one cruise-night diner owner said, "If you like it, we like it!"

Pro-Street

Pro-street cars are becoming more popular at cruise nights. A pro-street car is one that resembles the pro-stock race cars that compete at the drag strip. Pro-street cars can be built with any domestic or foreign car or truck. The overall look is extremely low, especially in the front.

The rear tires are up to 17 inches wide, like the slicks on a Funny Car. These large rear tires are contained within the car's original quarter panels. To accommodate the large rear tires, the rear of the car's frame is reworked and a pair of large sheet metal wheelhouses, called "tubs," are installed. The tubs occupy the space usually occupied by the car's back seat.

The interior of a pro-street car closely resembles that of a race car. Roll bars are installed and some owners even install a full roll cage. Some owners strip the interior to the basics—a seat and a few competition-style gauges. Others improve upon the original interior by adding finely trimmed seats and digital instruments. A large tachometer is prominently mounted on the instrument panel and competition-style, five-point seatbelts are installed.

Under the large hood scoop is an engine of monumental proportions. Big-block Chevy engines are the most popular, but anything goes when it comes to pro-street power. There are no rules or restrictions for pro-street engines. You will see an engine detailed to perfection and loaded with every horsepower-yielding accessory available.

The engine is a full-race Chevy big block with a tunnel-ram intake manifold, dual quads, and a scoop that sticks through the hood.

As you can tell from the smile on this driver's face, you don't have to own a high-dollar custom or hot rod to enjoy cruise night. An old Ford sedan in black primer with some hand-painted red and yellow flames on the front is great for cruising. This owner did spend a few dollars, however, for the flame-thrower tailpipes.

Lots of chrome and polished aluminum is the norm.

Pro-street cars are expensive to build and, in most cases, difficult to drive on the street. Their body and paint work is always outstanding, featuring special colors and graphics. Pro-street cars are the closest thing to a pure drag racing car that can be driven legally on the street. One thing about pro-street cars, they always draw a crowd at a cruise night.

Street Machines

Street machines represent the largest category of cars attending a cruise night. The street machine is generally a 1949-1972 car with a stock body or a mildly customized

Two cruise-night spectators take more than a passing interest in this beautifully restored 1936 LaSalle. *Hans Halberstadt*

body. It will probably have mag wheels and nonstock tires. The interior may be completely stock or may be modified. The engine will definitely not be stock. It may have some chrome dress-up accessories, but the intent of the engine modifications is to increase performance and reliability. Older, less-powerful engines may have been changed to a more modern small block.

Cruise nights bring out the best the American automotive enthusiast has to offer. Whether it's stock, modified, or a beater, the fun is being there and showing off what you own. As one car owner said, "I don't care if I win a trophy or not at a car show. The best 'trophies' I receive are the friendly waves, smiles, and thumbs-up from the general public when I'm driving my car down the road."

The interior of this pro-street 1957 Pontiac is typical of the quality of workmanship and detail owners put into their creations. The blue lights glowing in the instrument panel are the digital gauges. The Pontiac Indian Chief's profile has been milled out of the trick aluminum insert on the instrument panel.

This chopped red Chevy pickup is sandwiched between two stock Ford pickups. The Chevy's hood has been removed so everyone can see the blown big-block Chevy engine.

Cruising in a completely stock Model T Ford touring car can be as much fun as a new Corvette. Keep in mind that some of the hottest T-buckets seen at cruise nights started from a vehicle like this.

Luxury convertibles from the 1950s, like this 1956 Buick, have a lot of appeal for cruisers. They have excellent styling, powerful engines, and lots of room. This owner added a set of Roadmaster chrome wire wheels and pair of fuzzy dice to the mirror for that final nostalgic touch.

The big smile on the face of the owner of this El Camino says, "Yeah, I'm havin' a great time!" Along with the beautiful red paint job, this happy owner has added some subtle touches. Tasteful graphics along the side and billet mag wheels make his El Camino stand out from the others.

Fuzzy Dice

Fuzzy dice seem to be hanging from the mirrors of just about every car that cruises today. They come in all sizes and in colors to match any interior. When you ask the owner of fuzzy dice why they have them, they will usually reply that everybody had them in the 1950s and 1960s. Well, not quite everybody. If you were to pick up a hot rod magazine from the 1950s, you would be hard pressed to find a car with dice hanging from the mirror. Finding an ad for fuzzy dice in an enthusiast magazine back then was rare, too. J. C. Whitney listed them as "Giant Dice," for $1.49 postpaid in their 1962 mail-order catalog. Whitney touted them as the "biggest novelty since foxtails." J. C. Whitney also sold a variety of automotive novelty accessories like the Lucky 8-Ball Gear Shift Knob, the Cattle Caller Horn, and the Shaggy Rear Deck Mat. So, just how did this fuzzy dice thing start anyway?

This tradition seems to be an outgrowth of hanging baby shoes from the rearview mirror. This fad from the 1940s and 1950s was reserved for young married couples whose little baby boomer had outgrown his first pair of baby shoes. Fuzzy dice filled the gap for those couples who were just dating. It was a symbol of their "couplehood." The dice were made by the girlfriend of the guy who owned the car. They were constructed from angora yarn wrapped around a square block of foam or cardboard. This same angora yarn was wrapped around the guy's oversize class ring the girl wore on her finger. I have been told, but can't confirm, that fuzzy dice were first seen in California. The popularity of fuzzy dice waned in the 1960s when the rubber shrunken head became a popular item.

Nowadays, fuzzy dice can be ordered by the truckload in every size and color combination. At larger car shows and cruises there will probably be someone in a booth selling fuzzy dice and other 1950s novelties.

Today, fuzzy dice have become a statement by the owners that their car, and their attitude, is clearly 1950s.

CHAPTER 6

BLOCKBUSTER CRUISES

Each year several large car cruising events take place across the country. The two that seem to draw the most enthusiasm—not only for the cars, but for the romance of the road on which they are held—are the Woodward Avenue Dream Cruise and the Route 66 Rendezvous. These two events each draw more than 2,000 cars and hundreds of thousands of spectators. Everyone comes to celebrate the road and the vehicles that made these stretches of highway legendary.

Woodward Dream Cruise

Woodward Avenue was the Mecca of Midwestern cruising and street racing in the 1950s and 1960s. Its wide and smoothly paved surface with long sections of arrow-straight road between traffic signals provided the perfect location for what was affectionately known as stop-light-grand-prix racing.

In the late 1950s and early 1960s, Corvettes were the kings of Woodward. This 1960 with dual four-barrel carbs shows its stuff on the fabled street. *Tom Shaw*

79

A Super Sport Chevelle sits out the heavy Woodward Avenue traffic. Thousands of cars jam more than eight miles of Woodward Avenue for this annual event that brings out every imaginable type of vehicle to celebrate one of the most famous cruising streets in America. *Tom Shaw*

The profusion of hot factory iron churned out by Detroit engineers in the 1960s was drawn to Woodward like a magnet. If you lived in the Detroit area in the 1960s and wanted to drag race, Woodward Avenue was the place to go.

Woodward Avenue runs in a north-northwesterly direction from downtown Detroit through the cities of Detroit's northern suburbs. The Woodward cruising strip started in the city of Ferndale, between the intersections of 9 Mile and 10 Mile roads. It continued north through Pleasant Ridge, Huntington Woods, and Royal Oak.

In the 1950s and 1960s the main attraction in that area of Woodward was the Totem Pole drive-in restaurant. The Totem Pole was a mandatory cruise location. It was virtually impossible to find an open parking slot at the Totem Pole during prime cruising hours. If you were lucky enough to find a space, you would order a 65-cent Big Chief Burger.

From the Totem Pole, the cruise north passed several coffee shops as you crossed 12 Mile Road, Coolidge, and 13 Mile Road. The north end of the strip was marked by Ted's Drive-in at Square Lake Road in Birmingham. If you hadn't found a race on your northern pass on Woodward, either you weren't looking for one or it must have been raining. The trip south featured passes through the parking lots at Maverick's and the Elias Brother's Big Boy drive-ins in Royal Oak. What would you do when you got to the south end at your starting point in Ferndale? Turn around and cruise north again.

The proliferation of drive-ins, coffee shops, and diners dotting Woodward allowed for plenty of drive-in cruising and lots of spectating. Many small parking lots paralleled Woodward. These lots were used by Woodward cruisers and racers as a place to stop and discuss the race they just had, or were about to have, or just to watch the cars go by. Local police got wise and started to ticket the cruisers for "loitering" in those lots. Some of the brightest and best engineers working at GM and Chrysler lived in these northern suburbs. It wasn't unusual to see one of the factory race cars that would be tearing up Detroit Dragway on Sunday cruising Woodward on Fri-

Duggan's Irish Pub has become the unofficial host location along Woodward Avenue. Grandstands were erected for spectators to view cars as they passed by. Duggan's also hosted the local ABC television affiliate for a one-hour live broadcast during the 1996 cruise. *Tom Shaw*

day or Saturday night. Dick Keinath, now a retired Chevrolet engine engineer whose name appears on the patents of Chevy's big-block engine, cruised Woodward in the 1950s and 1960s. Keinath took delivery of his brand-new 1956 Chevy in December of 1955. Two days later he stood ankle deep in snow tearing the engine apart to install a hot cam so he could race on Woodward.

When the 1960s rolled around, the Big Three auto makers were each cranking out contenders for the drag strip super stock title. Mopar had its ram-inducted Max Wedge

cars; Pontiac had its Super Duty 421; Chevrolet its 409; and Ford its 406 and 427. Fully lettered, factory-prepared race cars occasionally appeared at the drive-ins on Woodward. Detroit was the birthplace of the musclecar, and Woodward was its playground. Win on Sunday—or on Woodward—and sell on Monday was a well-known axiom among Detroit's auto executives. I can't imagine John DeLorean getting the inspiration for the GTO while poring over spreadsheets in his mahogany-paneled executive office at GM. Designers and engineers got their inspiration

An occasional break in traffic allowed a GTO and a 'Cuda to relive the good old days of racing on Woodward Avenue. Traffic was so congested there were more overheated motors than races. *Tom Shaw*

and adrenaline on Woodward Avenue.

Woodward was overrun with Corvettes in the 1960s. Ted's Drive-in in Birmingham was the place to see Corvettes. Many GM executives lived in Birmingham and either owned a Corvette or were able to borrow a company car. Don Novak, now a Commander with the Royal Oak, Michigan, Police Department, remembers cruising Woodward in one of Chevrolet's Mako Shark Corvette prototypes. "The father of a friend of mine

was a Chevrolet executive and always had a Corvette," said Novak. "One day he brought home a Mako Shark, and of course, we went cruisin' on Woodward." Dave Holls was a Chevrolet stylist in the early 1960s who worked on the design of the then-new 1963 Corvette Sting Ray. Two days prior to the car's first public appearance, he had a chance to take one home. "I headed for Ted's Drive-in on Woodward Avenue," said Holls. "I pulled in with that coupe and every car in the

The Hemi-powered Silver Bullet was the fastest car ever to race on Woodward. Its reputation reached the West Coast, where hard-core street racers spoke with respect about Jimmy Addison's 1967 Dodge GTX. *Tom Shaw,* Muscle Car Review

place emptied to get a closer look."

In the early 1960s Cokes were 10 cents each and gas was 26 cents a gallon. A night of cruising on Woodward might cost only a couple of dollars. Customer turnover in the drive-ins was slow, as cruisers would arrive early and order a minimum amount of food. An experienced cruiser could nurse a 10-cent Coke and a small order of fries for more than an hour. Although the parking spaces were filled, the food was not being sold at a pace to pay the restaurant's expenses. Many Woodward drive-ins banned cruising, set time limits for patrons, or closed their doors. By that

time the musclecar era had come to a close. Higher gas prices, the Vietnam War, and soaring insurance premiums brought down the curtain on cruising Woodward Avenue.

In 1995, at the urging of Ferndale resident Nelson House, the cities along Woodward Avenue got together to re-create those golden days of cruising. They scheduled a one-day cruise event billed as the Woodward Dream Cruise. It was a phenomenal success with estimates of more than 4,000 cars and 250,000 spectators. Woodward Avenue was jammed with legions of overheating musclecars and hot rods all wanting to be part of the

Small parking lots are found all along Woodward Avenue in front of the businesses that line the street. In the 1950s and 1960s, racers would stop to hang out in these lots, where they would plan or discuss races. Others would simply park there to watch the ongoing car show. During the 1996 Woodward Dream Cruise, these lots again hosted spectators and impromptu car shows. *Tom Shaw*

show. The Royal Oak Police Department handed out souvenir drag racing tickets dated 1962. Hot cars were lined up bumper to bumper for miles, unable to drag race in a traffic jam.

In 1996 the scene was re-created with more cars (some estimates were as high as 10,000) and twice the number of spectators as the year before. Each city along Woodward hosted a car show with nostalgic rock bands and family-oriented events. Impromptu burnouts were almost as common as orders for hamburgers, fries, and a Coke. Some police looked the other way, but some did not—writing real tickets to unruly offenders. Even though the classic drive-ins were gone, Woodward was the same stretch of black top and the excitement was in the air. The local

ABC television affiliate did a one-hour live broadcast, including coverage from a helicopter sky-cam.

One of the featured cars at the 1996 Woodward Dream Cruise was the Silver Bullet: a Hemi-powered 1967 Dodge GTX. The Silver Bullet was the fastest street racer ever to lay parallel black streaks on Woodward. It was built by Jimmy Addison to be the ultimate street racer—and it was. Its reputation even reached the West Coast where on the corner of Devonshire and Sepulveda, Los Angeles' fastest street racers spoke about the Silver Bullet with the esteem it was due. Its Hemi engine boasted more than 490 cubic-inches and the silver-painted body had every lightweight part listed in the Mopar catalog. The rear fenders were slightly flared to

Musclecars like this Dodge Challenger RT were once the mainstay of cruising on Woodward Avenue. If it was fast, it cruised Woodward. *Tom Shaw*

accommodate racing slicks, and it ran a full exhaust system. Challengers brought their race cars in on trailers to take their best shot at the Silver Bullet, only to be defeated.

The Woodward Dream Cruise turns back the clock to the glory days of street racing and cruising for fun. Tom Shaw, editor of *Muscle Car Review* magazine, said, "If Disney were to make a musclecar theme park, it would have to be a re-creation of Woodward Avenue. But on Woodward, there was no admission. Just bring your car and take your best shot."

Route 66 Rendezvous

The annual Route 66 Rendezvous celebrates the most famous road in America. Its place in history is so revered that it became known as the "Mother Road."

Route 66 gained fame as the 2,400-mile highway connection from Chicago to the Pacific Ocean. It was opened in 1926, spanning three time zones and eight states. Songwriter Bobby Troupe was inspired in 1946 to write the now-famous lyrics while on a road trip along Route 66. It was first recorded by Nat King Cole and has since been recorded by more than 40 different artists. The romance of Route 66 was best epitomized in the TV show of the same name. In that series, Todd and Buzz cruised the fabled highway, chasing adventure in a Corvette. Today most of the original Route 66 has been bypassed with Interstate 40, but it has not been forgotten in San Bernardino.

San Bernardino contains several famous sites with cruising roots. One of these is the site of the first McDonald's restaurant. In 1940

Court Street in downtown San Bernardino is the center of activity for the annual Route 66 Rendezvous. Thousands of people line the street to watch the endless parade of rolling and rumbling sculpture.

Dick and Maurice McDonald opened their first drive-in at 14th and E streets. In 1948 the brothers abandoned carhop service for walk-up counter service. A hamburger was only 15 cents, and business was brisk. There were more than 200 McDonald's restaurants open in 1961 when the brothers sold to Ray Kroc. Today a small plaque commemorates the location, now home to the business offices of the San Bernardino Light Opera.

In 1990, Dan Stark Jr., the executive director of San Bernardino's Convention and Visitors Bureau, organized a local car show that included a cruise along one of the city's downtown streets. That show drew 300 cars and an estimated 4,000 spectators. In 1992 the event was moved to the downtown area to celebrate the 66th anniversary of Route 66 and attracted more than 700 vehicles and 100,000 spectators. The 1996 event topped all expectations with more than 1,700 registered cars and 200,000 spectators. In 1997 over 2,200 cars cruised San Bernadino's streets.

San Bernardino knows how to put on an automotive extravaganza. It begins by blocking out more than 11 square blocks of San Bernardino's downtown area just for cruisers. If you're not registered, you can't enter. The only cars allowed are pre-1973 American or foreign classics and all American sports cars or motorcycles. The city streets are turned into a one-way cruise route through the downtown area. Along the streets, participant's cars are backed into parking spaces at an angle. Bleachers for spectators are set up along Court Street to view this endless parade of rolling sculpture. Participants who are not cruising break out their beach chairs

The zoomie headers on Ken Asche's 1970 Camaro shot flames 10-feet high as he cruised the streets of San Bernardino during the 1996 Route 66 Rendezvous. Asche's Camaro runs on alcohol and will burn as much as 17 gallons during one 2 1/2-mile circuit.

Some things never change—guys in Corvettes *always* get the pretty girls. Corvettes are one of the more popular cars at the Route 66 cruise.

to sit near their car and watch the cars and the people go by.

And what goes by is one of the most amazing rolling automotive shows on earth. It's not just a hot rod show, it's a little of everything. Steve Long, a first-time participant in the 1996 event with his 1967 Corvette coupe, said, "There's everything and anything here: roadsters, high-boys, low-boys, restorations, and customs, and everybody is friendly." Cars come from neighboring states, Canada, and as far away as Ohio to cruise downtown "San Berdoo." Trophies are given to cruising participants only. Those who sit by their car all weekend will enjoy the show, but won't win any of the awards.

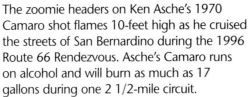

This slammed 1939 Buick was one of the most popular cars at the 1996 Route 66 Rendezvous.

Corvette owners take a break from cruising San Bernardino's streets to watch a restored 1962 Dodge convertible drive by.

Law enforcement takes a relaxed view, ignoring excessive noise, seatbelt use, and violations of motorcycle helmet laws. They are there to protect the public, but for the most part, they are delighted spectators. The San Bernardino Police Department motor unit shows its enthusiasm by decorating the front fenders of their Kawasaki police motorcycles with flames.

Saturday is the biggest day of the weekend, featuring the poker run, the open-header cruise and contest, and the burnout contest. The poker run, which is open to all participants, is a 32-mile driving event that requires participants to reach numerous checkpoints and draw a playing card at each stop. The card is recorded on a form the participant carries. At the end of the run, the participant with the best poker hand is the winner.

The open-header cruise lets participants drive the cruise route with headers or exhaust cutouts open. Cruising with the headers open guarantees lots of engine revving, to the delight of the crowd gathered at every corner. One stop along the drive is set up for the open-header contest. The Route 66 organizers set up a decibel meter about 30 feet from the cruise route. The cars are stopped near the microphone and given the signal to crank it up. As the driver revs the

The open-header cruise runs all afternoon on Saturday. Cars are allowed to cruise the city streets with open exhaust and are encouraged to participate in the eardrum-splitting open-header contest. The female passenger in this T-bucket is dealing with the noise to the best of her ability.

Even the San Bernardino Police Department's Motor Unit gets into the swing of things by adding flames to the front fenders of their Kawasaki motorcycles.

What could be more fun than cruising the streets of San Bernardino in a T-bucket? Spectators were lined up 10 deep along Court Street cheering their approval of every car that passed.

T-buckets generally seat two very snugly. How did these four young ladies squeeze into this hot rod?

engine, the crowd cheers, hoots, and waves raised fists in a circular motion, urging the driver to get a few extra revs out of his engine. The participant with the highest decibel reading wins. The loudest cars can push the needle into the range from 100 to 110-plus. It's a guy thing—lots of noise, smoke, and a few thrown fan belts.

The burnout contest is another male ritual with lots of smoke and noise. This event is held away from the crowded downtown streets to avoid any pesky insurance problems. The premise is simple: rev up your engine, pop the clutch, and let your tires smoke. The longest burn is the winner. How long is long? The 1996 winner smoked his tires to the delight of the crowd and a nearby tire dealer for more than a minute and a half.

The car that drew the most attention at the 1996 Route 66 Rendezvous was Ken Asche's 1978 Camaro. Ken's Camaro would attract attention anywhere because of its red paint, white flames, and aggressive stance. But when he cruised, people came running to see the fire show created by the zoomie headers protruding through the Camaro's hood. It is equipped with a small-block Chevy engine that runs on alcohol—lots of alcohol. In fact, Ken goes through 160 gallons of the stuff in a weekend. "I burn between 7 and 17 gallons of alcohol in one circuit (about 2.5 miles) of the town," Asche said. It's the Chevy engine's 13:1 compression, roller cam, and fat mixture that provides the pyrotechnics. The crowds around Ken's Camaro required a police motorcycle escort to keep the people back. Everyone loved it. When asked which car was his favorite, 81-year-old spectator Fred Yurk of Ripin, Wisconsin, said, "I like the one with the fire comin' out."

All types of vehicles come out to cruise the streets of San Bernardino during the Route 66 Rendezvous. This slammed Chevy truck sports a highly polished set of Z/28 wheels.

The Woodward Dream Cruise and Route 66 Rendezvous epitomize the love Americans have for their cars and for the freedom of the road. These events celebrate a car culture that is uniquely American.

Several police departments brought their restored police cars and cruised the streets with sirens blaring and red lights flashing.

Roller Rita

*R*ita Evans Scharnhorst is crazy about the 1950s. She was born into the era, but had to wait until the 1990s to relive some of her best memories. Rita first swiveled her way into the 1950s as the Idaho State Hula Hoop Champion of 1970. Today "Roller Rita" is one of the most recognizable personalities at car shows in and around the Seattle-Tacoma area. She puts a smile on the face of anyone who sees her coming across the parking lot on a pair of roller skates, balancing a tray of sodas in one hand. Roller Rita is a "freelance carhop."

As a lover of all things from the 1950s, Rita had always enjoyed attending car events and cruise nights. But she sensed something was missing. In 1995, she voiced her opinion to the owner of a local cruise-night hangout: "You need a carhop!"

The owner was doubtful at first of Rita's ability to navigate in and out of his diner on roller skates, while trying to balance a tray of food. But Rita pulled off her first 1950s time-warp gig in fine fashion, became a local celebrity, and kick-started her new career as a freelance carhop. Today, Rita appears as a working carhop at 50 car shows and cruise nights each year.

There are some hazards to this line of work. "It's a good thing I have a loud whistle," Rita says, describing an incident at a cruise night when a cruiser accidentally backed into her. And once she unknowingly lost a toe-stop off one of her roller skates. Her stop was less than graceful as she flailed off-balance for a second or two, but she didn't fall or spill her tray of food.

Roller Rita's presence at cruise night is a perfect fit—like an ice-cold mug of A&W root beer in your hand. Wearing her adorable pink costume and genuine smile, she represents everything good and wholesome that we remember from the days when teenagers worked as carhops in diners across America.

INDEX